GROUP RULES!

The Social Skills and Ground Rules for Children's Groups

Sherry Henig, Ph.D.

Illustrations by Jeff Plotkin

Brenner
publishing

Long Island, NY

The Purpose of this Book

Lots of children belong to groups. There are play groups and friendship groups. There are church groups and social skills groups. There are also groups for children with special concerns. For example, there are Banana Splits groups for children whose parents are separated or divorced and bereavement groups for children whose loved one has died. Girl scout troops and boy scout troops are groups too.

One of the things that children's groups have in common is that the children in them, like you and the other children in your group, have a chance to interact, or socialize, with other children during group meetings.

Social skills are basically the rules that tell people the best ways to interact, or socialize, with others. And ground rules help everyone in a group do this in an organized way so that the group runs smoothly and everyone gets along.

On the next page, you will read a list of social skills and ground rules for groups. You will also have a chance to add more rules if you and the other members of your group would like. (And, of course, you and the others can take out rules that do not apply to *your* group.)

The rest of this book will help you learn all about these different skills and rules. And you will have a chance to see how the children in Ms. Dorothy's group learn them.

By the time Ms. Dorothy's group meeting is over, all the children in her group will have learned the rules. And they will have made friends, and will have had a great time.

Once you start to use the social skills and ground rules in your group, you'll make some great friends and you will have a great time too.

Kim

Tameeka

Derrick

Ms. Dorothy

Nilda

Ethan

Matthew

Abigail

Social Skills
and Ground Rules

Name_____

- **Arrive on Time and Greet Everyone**
- **Be Kind to New Members**
- **Make Eye Contact with Others When You are Speaking**
- **Keep Your Comments Brief When You Are Speaking**
- **Show Concern for the Speaker When You Are Listening**
- **Only One Listener Can Speak at a Time**
- **Share the Toys and Agree on Which Game to Play**
- **Agree on the Rules Before You Start to Play a Game**
- **Be a Good Sport**
- **Stay Calm No Matter How You Feel**
- **Mind Your Manners**
- **Help Clean Up**
- **Say "Goodbye"**

What other rules would be good for *your* group?

_____

_____

Arrive On Time And Greet Everyone

It is important to come to your group meeting on time. And, when you enter the room, it is proper to greet everyone.

When you and the other group members greet one another, it will help all of you feel like you care about one another.

Also, when everyone greets one another, it helps you and the others feel that you belong to something special.

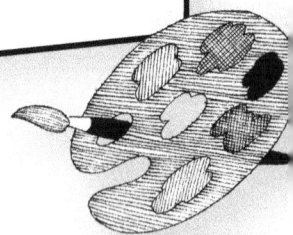

Arrive On Time And Greet Everyone

Ms. Dorothy is pleased that everyone arrived on time and is greeting one another.

Be Kind
To New Members

Remember that the new members that come to your group may not know anyone. Also, they may not know what happens in the group. So they may be feeling shy or scared or confused.

It is important to be considerate and help them feel comfortable.

Introducing yourself to a new member might help them feel more comfortable.

You could also ask them if they would like to sit next to you.

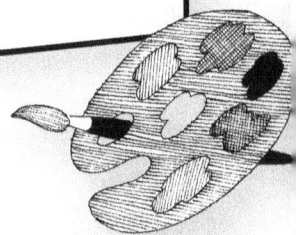

Be Kind To New Members

Nilda is feeling more comfortable now that Derrick has introduced himself to her. It also helps that the others are smiling at her.

Make Eye Contact With Others When You Are Speaking

Y ou need to remember a lot of things when you are talking to a group. Make sure to look at everyone, not just the leader.

If you look at your friends in the group, they will feel that you care about them, and about their reactions to what you are saying.

Also, when you look at the others in the group while you are talking you will be able to see if anyone is losing interest in what you are talking about. If your friends in the group lose interest and become bored, they will not have a good time. Also, if they are losing interest they will not act like they care about what you are talking about. That will make it hard for you to have a good time.

You can tell if someone might be losing interest if they are looking away, or if they are yawning or talking to a friend.

Also, they might be losing interest if they are wiggling in their chair. (Or they might just have to go to the bathroom.)

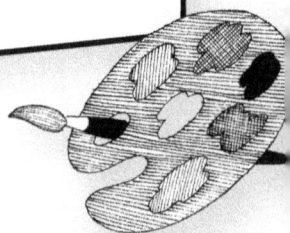

Make Eye Contact With Others When You Are Speaking

Tameeka's looking right at Derrick. She can tell that he is interested because he is looking right back at her. But Tameeka isn't looking at Abigail and Kim, so she can't see that they are whispering to one another. They might have lost interest in what Tameeka is talking about.

Keep Your Comments Brief When You Are Speaking

Remember to keep your comments brief when you are speaking to the group. When you speak for short periods of time, you give the others a chance to ask questions. You also give yourself a chance to see if anyone is starting to lose interest.

Also, keep in mind that other children in the group may want a chance to talk too.

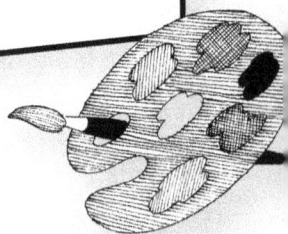

Keep Your Comments Brief When You Are Speaking

Tameeka is being considerate of the others by keeping her comments brief, and by asking if the others would like a chance to talk.

Show Concern For The Speaker When You Are Listening

The listeners in a group have things to remember just like the speakers do. When you are the listener, it is kind to show that you care about the speaker's feelings. You show that you care when you ask the speaker questions.

If the speaker has said something that made them proud, you could show you care by complimenting them.

If the speaker tells the group about something that made them sad, you could show you care by saying something sympathetic.

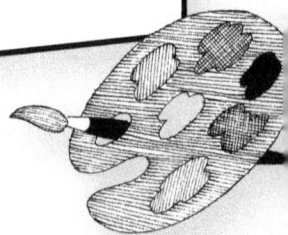

Show Concern For The Speaker When You Are Listening

Tameeka is showing interest and concern by asking Ethan a question.
Others could show concern with comforting words.
They could say, "I'm sorry your homework is making you so unhappy."

Only One Listener Can Speak At a Time

When you are the listener, you need to remember to wait your turn and not interrupt.

You can raise your hand to let others know that you would like a chance to talk.

Or you can wait for a pause in the conversation, say, "Excuse me," and then you can start to talk.

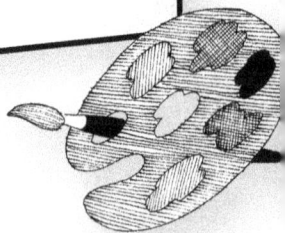

Only One Listener Can Speak At a Time

Abigail raised her hand and said, "Excuse me." Everyone else stopped talking. Now that she sees that she can take a turn to talk, Abigail is offering to help Ethan with his homework.

Share The Toys And Agree On Which Game To Play

If you decide to play with toys during playtime, then remember to share them with others.

If you want to play a game, then remember that you and the others will have to agree on which game to play.

If everyone cannot decide on which game to play, then the group could vote and the majority could rule.

If there is no majority, the group needs to try some other way to figure out what to play.

You could try a counting game like one-potato two-potato. Or you could draw straws.

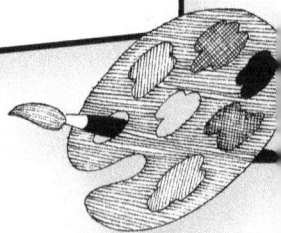

14

Share The Toys And Agree On Which Game To Play

Nilda would like to do a puzzle and Abigail would like to play a board game.
They're doing rock, paper, scissors to figure out which one they'll do.
Tameeka is practicing a coin toss, just in case she is needed to help break a tie.

Agree On The Rules Before You Start to Play a Game

If the group decides to play a game, then everyone has to agree on the rules. Reading the instructions can help.
(Of course it is hard to read the instructions if they have gotten lost.)

If everyone cannot agree on the rules, then maybe the group can come up with a compromise.

Here is one compromise: you and the others can play it one way the first time, and another way the next time.

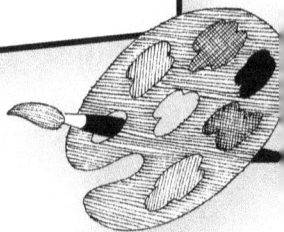

Agree On The Rules Before You Start to Play a Game

Ms. Dorothy's group found a game that had the instructions printed on the inside of the box top. Kim and Nilda are holding up the box top so everyone can read the instructions.

Be A Good Sport:
Bragging winners and sore losers are not good sports.

A bragging winner acts like a show-off when they win and a sore loser gets too upset when they lose.

It is important not to be a bragging winner or a sore loser. Bragging winners and sore losers make other people feel uncomfortable.

Sometimes people do not even want to play with a sore loser or a bragging winner.

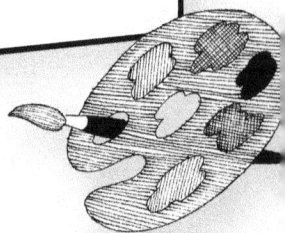

Be A Good Sport:
Bragging winners and sore losers are not good sports.

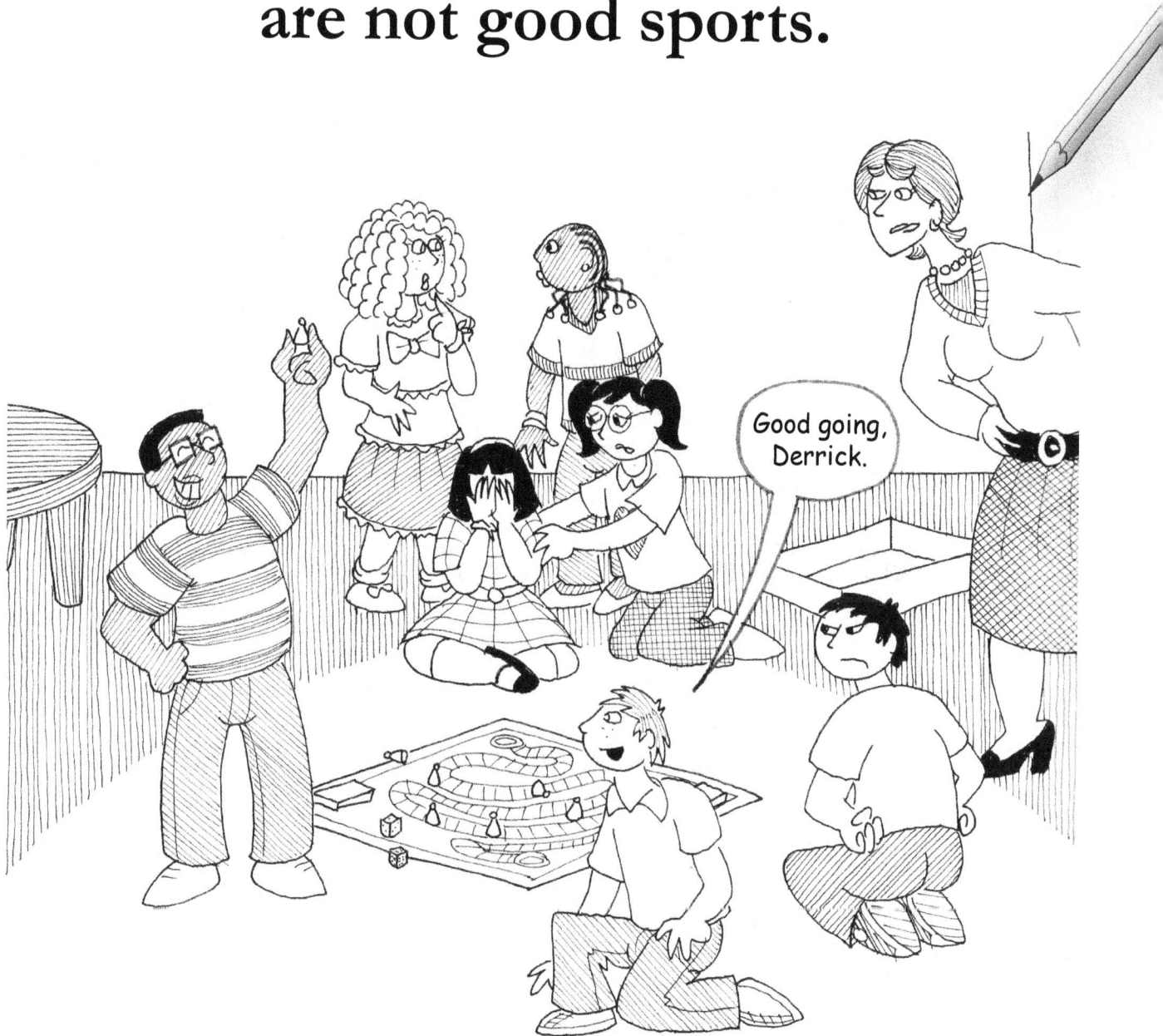

Good going, Derrick.

Kim is crying because she lost. Abigail and Tameeka don't know what to say to her. They think she is acting a little immature. Matthew is upset that he lost, too. He thinks Derrick is bragging and he feels like hitting him. Even though he lost, Ethan is trying to be a good sport. He's congratulating Derrick.

Stay Calm No Matter How You Feel

Sometimes things happen in a group that might make you angry. It is important to use your words when you get angry, and not your hands.

And angry words that are thoughtful are better than angry words that are insulting.

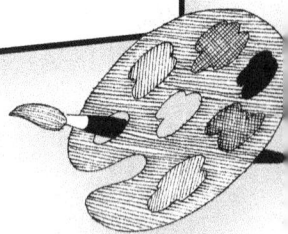

Stay Calm No Matter How You Feel

Matthew is trying to stay calm and control his anger at Derrick.
He's using his words and not his hands. Derrick is surprised.
He didn't realize that he looked like he was bragging.

Mind Your Manners

It is good manners to apologize to someone when you hurt their feelings. Also, remember not to burp or belch on purpose. And do not pick your nose. Use a tissue if you feel you must take care of your nose.

And remember, use a napkin if you ate a snack and have food on your face. (Food goop on a person's face is not a pretty sight.)

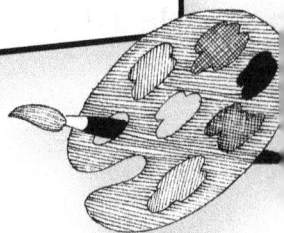

Mind Your Manners

I'm sorry if I acted like I was bragging.

Derrick is apologizing for acting like he was bragging. Matthew has decided to be more considerate of Derrick's feelings. He is congratulating him for winning the game. Tameeka has decided to comfort Kim by giving her a tissue so that she can wipe her tears and blow her nose.

Help Clean Up

The people who will be using the room after you will appreciate a clean room. So you need to help clean up the group room when it is almost time to leave.

If you do your part to help out, the other children who are cleaning will think that you care about their feelings.

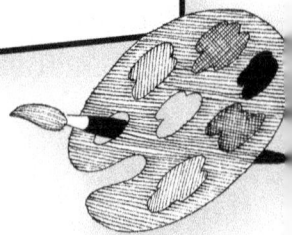

Help Clean Up

Tameeka is annoyed that Nilda and Kim are not helping to clean up.

Say "Goodbye"

Saying "goodbye" when you leave is just as important as saying "hello" when you arrive. So say something thoughtful when you leave your friends at the end of your group meeting.

"Goodbye" or "See you soon" are two things that you could say to the others.

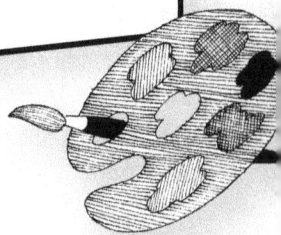

Say "Goodbye"

More Social Skills and Ground Rules

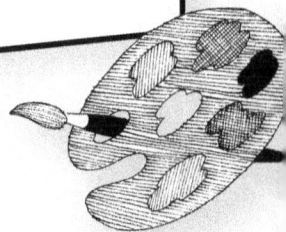

_____

_____

_____

More Social Skills and Ground Rules

Ms. Dorothy is telling everyone another rule. Derrick and Matthew think it's a really good idea. What other ideas do you have for *your* group?

ISBN13: 978-0-9777203-5-4
ISBN10: 0-9777203-5-7
Library of Congress Control Number: 2008936074
Cataloging in Publication Data on file with publisher.

Brenner Publishing, LLC
P. O. Box 584
Hicksville, New York 11802-0584
(516) 433-0804
Email: info@BrennerPublishing.com
www.BrennerPublishing.com

Illustrations: Jeff Plotkin
Book Design: Gary James Withrow
Production and Marketing: Concierge Marketing Inc.

Printed in the United States of America
2 3 4 5 6 7 8 9 10

www.ingramcontent.com/pod-product-compliance
Lightning Source LLC
Chambersburg PA
CBHW081549040426
42448CB00015B/3269